A Family in Hong Kong

LIBRARY OF CONGRESS CATALOGING-IN-PUBLICATION DATA

McKenna, Nancy Durrell.
    A family in Hong Kong.

    Summary: Describes the life of ten-year-old Tse Yik Ming who lives in an apartment
building in Hong Kong.
    1. Hong Kong—Social life and customs—Juvenile literature. 2. Family—Hong Kong—
Juvenile literature. [1. Family life—Hong Kong. 2. Hong Kong—Social life and customs.]
I. Title. II. Series.
DS796.H75M34   1987   951'.25   87-3475
ISBN 0-8225-1676-4 (lib. bdg.)

Manufactured in the United States of America

    2   3   4   5   6   7   8   9   10   97   96   95   94   93   92   91   90

A Family in Hong Kong

Nancy Durrell McKenna

Lerner Publications Company • Minneapolis

This is Tse Yik Ming. He is 10 years old and lives with his parents in Kowloon, Hong Kong.

This is how he writes his name in English and Chinese characters.

Yik   謝

Ming   易

Tse   明

Tse is his surname or family name. His first name, Yik Ming, is Cantonese for "thoughtful and understanding." His family speaks Cantonese at home. Most people in Hong Kong speak Cantonese, which is a Chinese language, but a lot of people speak English, too. Yik Ming is learning English at school.

The place where the Tses live, in Kowloon on the Kowloon Peninsula, got its name from an old Chinese legend. Kowloon means "nine dragons."

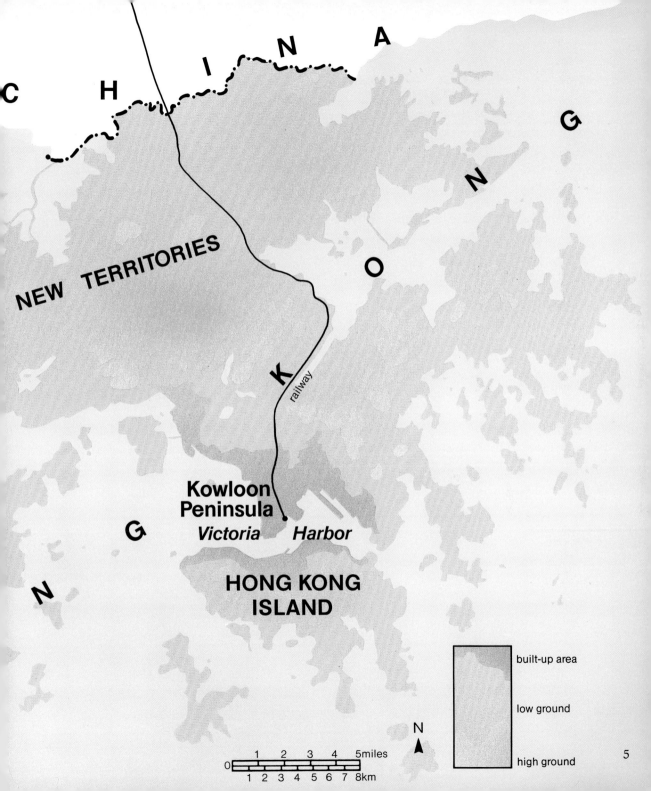

C H I N A

NEW TERRITORIES

K   railway

O   N   G

Kowloon
Peninsula

Victoria   *Harbor*

HONG KONG
ISLAND

G

N

N
▲

built-up area

low ground

high ground

	1	2	3	4	5miles
0					
1	2	3	4	5	6	7	8km

5

Hong Kong is made up of the Kowloon Peninsula, the New Territories, and Hong Kong Island, as well as 235 smaller islands.

Yik Ming's mother and father came from Kwangtung Province in southern China. Mr. Tse left China in 1959 because he didn't agree with the Cultural Revolution.

The Cultural Revolution happened when the Chinese leaders decided that scientists, teachers, artists, and others with special skills might become richer or more powerful than peasants and workers. This was against their Communist principles, which said everyone should be exactly equal. Some of these skilled or talented people were sent to work on farms or put in prison. In parts of the country there were riots and violence.

Lots of people came to Hong Kong then. Mr. Tse walked across the mountains of southern China to reach Hong Kong. Yik Ming's mother stayed behind in China until his father found a job and somewhere to live in Hong Kong.

In the beginning it was very hard. Mr. Tse says it was difficult to find a place to live. There wasn't enough housing for all the people who were arriving from China.

Now the Tses live on the Pak Tin Estate. Yik Ming likes it there. There's space to ride his bike and a playground. That's Yik Ming's best friend on the slide with him.

The Tses live on the seventh floor of a sixteen story building. When Yik Ming is feeling energetic, he uses the stairs. Usually he has his BMX bike with him, so he has to take the elevator.

There are a lot of high-rise buildings in Hong Kong because so much of the land is too wet or hilly to build on.

Mr. Tse says that a new apartment is completed every seven minutes. But there is still a long waiting list for the apartments. Yik Ming's parents had to wait ten years before they could move to their apartment.

The apartment is small and very cozy. There is a small kitchen, a living room, and a bedroom. Yik Ming sleeps in a bunk bed above his parents' double bed.

Sometimes Yik Ming's mother asks him to see if the washing has dried. The washing is hung out of the window on bamboo poles to dry. This saves a lot of space indoors, but they have to make sure that nothing falls off the poles.

One of Mr. Tse's friends from work is coming over this evening, so Yik Ming's mother is busy preparing dinner.

The pan she's using is called a *wok*. It's a very clever shape because when the wok is heated, the heat spreads up the sides of the bowl and all the food is cooked evenly. It can be used to steam food or to fry lots of different foods together.

While Yik Ming's mother puts some fresh fish and strips of ginger in the wok to steam, his father puts up the table and Yik Ming fetches the bowls, spoons, and chopsticks. The family is having creamed corn soup to begin with. Mr. Tse says that it's good to start a meal with soup because it helps you to digest your food.

By the time they've finished eating the soup, the fish is ready. As well as the steamed fish, there are chicken, crab, prawns, vegetables, and rice. Yik Ming thinks Mr. Fung should come over for dinner every day.

Yik Ming's school is a ten-minute walk from where he lives. He goes to the Buddhist Chan Sik Yam Primary School. You don't have to be Buddhist to go there, but quite a lot of the students are Buddhist.

Yik Ming goes to school from 8:00 A.M. to 12:45 P.M. every day, except Sunday. Another group of pupils has lessons from 1:00 P.M. to 5:45 P.M. Most primary schools have two sessions every day.

Yik Ming is in fifth grade. All his lessons except for English are taught in Cantonese. Some of the English words are very hard for him to say because the sounds are so different from Cantonese. But Yik Ming is good at writing in English.

In Hong Kong, many people speak English and the street signs are often written in both English and Chinese characters. Britain took control of Hong Kong Island in 1842 and Kowloon Peninsula in 1860 to settle disagreements with China about trade. Then in 1898 China leased the New Territories to Britain for 99 years.

Now Hong Kong is an important trading center. There are a lot of British and other foreign businesses here.

When the 99-year lease runs out on July 1, 1997, all of Hong Kong will be run by China again. Everyone says that there will be a lot of changes, but nobody seems to know exactly what they will be.

Yik Ming's class in school has a break in the middle of the morning. He usually brings a flask of soup for a snack to keep him going until it's time to go home.

On his way home from school, he treats himself to a stick of fish balls with his pocket money. The fish balls only cost HK$1 (one Hong Kong dollar). Chocolate bars cost about HK$4 because chocolate has to be imported from countries like Britain and the United States.

Yik Ming's allowance is HK$10 a week, but he saves some of it to buy scale model airplanes and cars.

In the evening, when Yik Ming has finished his home-work, he likes to watch television. There are four channels to choose from. Two channels are English and two are Chinese. A lot of the programs are foreign, but they are usually dubbed in Cantonese.

If there isn't anything he wants to see on television, Yik Ming might play with his computer game until 10:30 P.M., when it's time to go to bed.

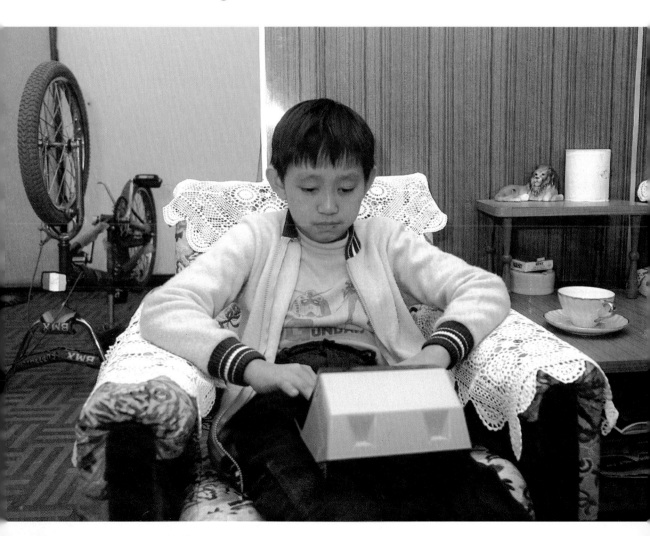

When Mr. Tse first came to Hong Kong, he found a job in a printing firm. Now he is a supervisor in a large printing company called Dai Nippon. They print books for publishers in a lot of countries, including Britain and the United States.

Mr. Tse's job is to supervise the bindery section. This is where the books are put together after they've been printed.

The books are printed on huge sheets of paper. Then the sheets have to be dried and folded. All the folded sections are stacked in order and stitched together. The edges are trimmed and, finally, a cover can be put on each book.

The pictures show some of the big machines that are used to fold, stitch, and trim the books. Part of Mr. Tse's job is to see that all of the machines are running properly.

Mr. Tse and his co-workers bring their lunches to work. Today their tablecloth is some spare sheets from a cookbook which is being printed.

Sunday is Mr. Tse's day off, and Yik Ming's too. The Tses usually go to a *dim sum* restaurant for lunch. Their favorite place is the Nam Chuk Restaurant.

The waitresses bring the dim sum around on big carts so the Tses can choose which ones they want. Yik Ming's favorite dim sum are *har kow* (steamed shrimp dumpling), *tsun guen* (deep-fried spring roll) and *nor mai chi* (coconut snowball).

Most dim sum are served in round baskets and can be ordered one at a time. At the end of the meal, the waitress adds up the number of baskets on the table to see how much the bill comes to.

The Tses have big pots of tea with their dim sum. Yik Ming's parents like to read the papers while they drink their tea. No one's in a hurry on Sundays and the waitresses don't mind how long they stay.

This afternoon, the Tses are going on a picnic to Kam Shun Park, but first they have to go to the market.

There are lots of markets all over Kowloon. Yik Ming's mother likes to go to different markets and sometimes to a supermarket. But the Pak Tin market is the most convenient.

Yik Ming's mother buys most of the family's food fresh every day. She knows a lot of the stall owners, so they give her good prices. Sometimes her shopping takes ages because she stops at all the stalls to chat. But today the Tses are in a hurry to get to the park.

20

After they have bought some oranges, the Tses go to the
meat stall which sells lots of different kinds of meats. They
have to buy some meat for a barbecue. Peking duck is one
of Yik Ming's favorite foods, but his mother says they can't
barbecue it because it's already cooked. She buys some hot
dogs or frankfurters for the barbecue. Then Mr. Tse and
Yik Ming help to carry the shopping home.

It's not very far to Kam Shun Park, so Mr. Tse says that Yik Ming can phone a taxi to take them there. Mr. Fung and his family are coming on the picnic with the Tses. The Tses will pick them up on the way.

There are lots of country parks around Kowloon and the New Territories, but Kam Shun is Yik Ming's favorite because it's a special reserve for monkeys. Yik Ming wants to give the monkeys some of their picnic, but there are signs asking visitors not to feed them.

In the middle of the park, there's a picnic area with barbecue pits for everyone to use. Mr. Tse lights a fire and they all watch to make sure that it's going properly. Yik Ming thinks it is very tricky to get the charcoal to the right heat for cooking.

When the charcoal is hot enough, they sit around the barbecue pit and cook their own food. Everyone grabs a barbecue fork and skewers some pieces of meat. The meat has been spread with sweet and spicy sauces. Then they hold the meat over the hot coals until it sizzles. By the time the meat is barbecued, the smell makes Yik Ming very hungry. He thinks it's worth waiting for.

Every year, Mr. Tse gets a week's holiday. He takes some days off to celebrate the New Year and saves two or three days so that he can go to visit the Tses' relatives in southern China.

Mr. Tse's parents still live in Kwangtung Province where he was born. Yik Ming's mother was born there too, and her father still lives there, but her mother died a few years ago.

On the first and fifteenth days of each month, the Tses light some incense at home to respect Grandmother's memory and to honor their ancestors. The flowers and oranges are to bring them good luck and prosperity.

Mr. Tse always takes some presents for his relatives in China when he visits them.

Yik Ming and his mother don't go to China because it's too expensive. But before Mr. Tse goes, he always takes them to visit Hong Kong Island and help him choose some presents.

There's a subway and a bus which go to Hong Kong Island through tunnels under the harbor. But it's more fun to go on the Star Ferry.

Inside the ferry terminal there are lots of people coming and going. The Tses have to be careful not to lose each other.

On the ferry, Yik Ming's parents find a seat but he likes to stand near the rail and watch the tankers and *sampans* in the harbor. Sampans are the flat-bottomed boats with sails in the picture. Some of the ships are on their way to China. Victoria Harbor is one of the busiest in the world.

There are so many shops in the Central District of Hong Kong Island that it's quite difficult to choose just a few presents.

There are big covered markets and shopping arcades, so you can spend hours window-shopping. Yik Ming's mother sometimes treats him to a chocolate bar for being patient.

Most people live out-
side the Central District
and come in to work or
to shop. The streets are
busy with visitors and
people going to their of-
fices, and there's always
a lot of traffic.

When the Tses have
finished their shopping,
they go to Victoria Peak.
The Peak Tram is a fu-
nicular railway or cable
railway. The cars are
pulled up the side of the
hill to Victoria Peak by
a cable.

The view from the top
is fantastic. Even the
high-rise buildings look
small. China looks a long
way away from here. It's
strange for Yik Ming to
think that his father will
be there soon. He would
like to go there with him
some day.

The Crowded Streets of Hong Kong

When the British gained control of Hong Kong it had only about 5,000 people. As a British territory, however, it became a refuge for the Chinese. Whenever political trouble and violence broke out in China, thousands of people fled to British-ruled Hong Kong.

By 1965, the population had grown to more than 3 million, and by 1980, it had reached about 5½ million. This rapid growth in population helped Hong Kong become a center of manufacturing as well as trade. There are always plenty of people to work in the factories and in commerce. "Made in Hong Kong" is a familiar stamp on products from clothing to toys to electronics.

The population growth has also caused problems for Hong Kong. Schools, housing, medical care, electrical services, and more must be provided for the floods of new residents who arrive daily.

Hong Kong has found many ways to solve these problems. For example, there is a shortage of land in Hong Kong, and much of the land is hilly or mountainous. The people of Hong Kong have solved this problem by putting up tall buildings, which hold more people. They build on the sides of the hills in Kowloon and Victoria, where some of the streets are so steep that they are made of stairs. They also make new land to build on. They carry rock and earth down from the mountains and dump it into the harbors to make firm ground. The airport in Kowloon is built out into the harbor on land created this way.

Facts about Hong Kong

Capital: Victoria

Languages: English and Chinese

Form of Money: Hong Kong dollar

Area: 1,126 square miles
(2,916 square kilometers)
    Only 410 square miles (1,061 square
    kilometers) is land.

Population: About 6 million
    On the average, about 14,000 people
    live in each square mile of Hong Kong
    (5,460 per square kilometer).

NORTH
AMERICA

SOUTH
AMERICA

EUROPE

A S I A

AFRICA

Hong Kong

AUSTRALIA

Families the World Over

Some children in foreign countries live like you do. Others live very differently. In these books, you can meet children from all over the world. You'll learn about their games and schools, their families and friends, and what it's like to grow up in a faraway land.

Lerner Publications Company, 241 First Avenue North, Minneapolis, Minnesota 55401

951
M

McKenna, Nancy
Durrell.

A family in Hong
Kong.

$15.95

DATE			